I'm Still Standing Here

By Candi Usher

Prologue

This is a unique book about Cherise. It is told in the first person as she retells her life story to the reader. She highlights her decisions and how they affected her and others around her. She finds herself in situations where critical choices are made for her, and she has to figure out if her decisions will make or break her. Despite the obstacles she faces in life, she keeps believing. Yet, she is caught up in bad choices and decisions. Can she be freed, or is she stuck for life?

Table of Contents

Prologue

Chapter One

Chapter Two

Chapter Three

Chapter Four

Chapter Five

Chapter Six

Chapter Seven

Chapter Eight

Epilogue

Get Help

Chapter One

Hello!! My name is Cherise. I'm 19, chocolate brown with the same color eyes, and I'm living a lie right now. I have to go back to the beginning so you can understand what I mean. I lived a great life growing up. My parents were married, we lived in a nice house, and extended family wasn't too far away. I played sports growing up. I could be a girly girl, but being a tomboy was life. Outside was everything to me. I have an annoying little brother (we're 18 months apart). I love him, yet he's the bane of my existence. Things were going well until my mom got sick. I didn't understand what was going on at first. I knew she had to go away for some time to get better. The first time was when I was around 12 or 13. It was extremely rough. Things were said that hurt, and I never truly got over them. I didn't have anyone to talk to. I was starting high school, so it was another change added to my already going crazy life.

High school started, and I made some new friends and even had a few boyfriends. One in particular was a guy who had been pursuing me since we were younger. He was a little older than me, but we finally got the chance to be together. It didn't last long because he eventually graduated. With my mom being sick, and feeling like I had no one to depend on because I had grown apart from so many people, I began to feel lonely.

Out of the blue, I met this amazing guy. I thought the attention he began paying me was so cute. With my mom being sick and having to take on extra responsibility, I just wanted someone to pay me attention. He did.

It started with his cousin coming to hang out with me. She would approach me and strike up a conversation. Every day she would come to talk to me. We became quick friends. Then she began bringing me notes that they were from a secret admirer. Y'all remember how we used to fold notes, then write the to and from on the outside so they could be identified. I wrote little notes back and passed them to him through her. I couldn't believe I had someone who was crushing on me. I was 16, but I wanted a longer-lasting relationship. Yes, I know now that that was foolish at such a young age. Yet, at that time, I wanted more comfort than anything with everything that was going on.

Anyways, back to this admirer. He was a great mystery to me. He said all the right things. He made me feel good just with his words. Then he began sending little bags of candy. That was the sweetest thing he could have done. I never had a man buy me anything other than my father. But my dad doesn't count because I'm forever a Daddy's girl. I'm a total sucker for a man who does just little important things for me. I felt so special and wondered when I would see my secret admirer. I wanted to know what he looked like, what he saw in me, and why he picked me. I didn't know he saw my weakness, my need for attention that I should have waited on. I didn't know that his thoughts and plans were nowhere near what mine were.

One day, I finally got to see his face. His cousin had come up to me and asked me to follow her. Around the corner stood a 5'9" handsome guy. His skin was a beautiful pecan tan and he had a somewhat muscular build. I could not believe he was my secret admirer. We started a conversation and found we had so many more things in common than what the notes said. I liked him so much. What I didn't know was that I wasn't the only girl he was giving notes to. As we began talking more and more, the more bad things I heard about him. I was told he already had a girlfriend. People told me they saw him with other girls. I didn't want to believe what I was hearing. There was no way he wanted anyone else but me. Because that's what HE told me. And I believed him.

I was a good girlfriend, and I should have been the only girl he wanted. I could change him. I knew I could. My love and feelings for him would do the job. One day, my brother was jumped. I didn't do anything. I wanted to jump in and protect my brother, but I was scared I was going to get hurt too. I thought my boyfriend would defend my brother. But he didn't. He laughed at what was happening. I figured it may have been a fluke, not knowing that he was the reason my brother was jumped, and that's why he was laughing. I still thought I could get him to change. I would stick with him and show him what life could be like if he changed. I didn't realize I was letting him change me, instead of exerting the "influence" I thought I had.

The next thing I knew, I found out that he was banned from the school. He wasn't even supposed to be on the property. I felt special that he would take a chance to see me even though he could get in trouble. My, how wrong I was. He would encourage me to skip school so I could come hang out with him. He was priming and prepping me for his next move. It was a setup, and I didn't even see the trap. I don't know how I passed

11th grade, but I did despite everything going on.

Chapter Two

My family life was starting to go crazy again. My mom was sick. Her health issues were impacting the whole family. My dad was working constantly, and my mom had to go to a hospital again, this time for a longer time. I took on the responsibility of my chores and cooking. On top of that, I had homework. I wanted to get away from it all. I told my boyfriend about my problems, and he gave me comfort. He kept encouraging me to go beyond kissing him, promising that he could help me forget the problems. He had been pushing and pushing for me to sleep with him. I would let him touch me more and more, not realizing the path I was running down. He broke my walls more and more. I trusted him so much that I gave him my one treasure. What I didn't know was that there was a bet on my virginity. I wish I knew then what I know now.

It was a special moment for me. It wasn't for him. He lied and said it was his first time too. The words that I know now were all lies. All that mattered to him was that he got in my pants. I was another girl he conquered. I was praying to God I wasn't pregnant because I didn't want to end high school like that. Fortunately, I didn't get pregnant from that encounter. I found out later that he wanted my virginity because that was the only type of girl he had never slept with. Yep. Way to feel special.

I believed that giving him something so special would change him. Yet, he remained the same. I would dedicate a song to him on the radio and turn around, and another girl would dedicate one to him too. I figured it was another guy with the same name so I brushed it off. I thought I was his only love. Yes, I'm aware of how naive I was. You try being a broken by that time 17-year-old. The only person who seemed to care about you was the very person who was hurting you. Yet, you would rather take that pain over the pain of a parent who told you to your face they no longer wanted you. That's the knife to the heart. When he offered me a way to get from home, I took it. I left home at 17. I thought I was leaving for the better, not knowing I was stepping into something so much worse.

He took me back to his parent's house. I had been to the house, but never inside of it. His mom was particular about it. I learned why. The house was dilapidated and appeared as if it could fall apart from a strong wind or rainstorm. I made my decision, though, and I was going to stick to it. I went to school from his house. My schedule had me in school for half a day as a senior to leave at the end of the classes. Instead of taking that opportunity to do something productive and running with it, I flushed it down the toilet. I used to dream of attending Florida

State University, but I killed that dream with my choices and decisions.

I figured by skipping school, I could get a job and start saving money to get us a place. He got me a job at the place he worked. I liked that we worked together and could go home together. Yet, he was still playing games. I started going back to school. The next thing I know, this girl begins appearing at our job. She was about 6'1". She had dark skin. To me, her hair was awful. That was just me, though.

I didn't know who she was, but I didn't feel right about her.

    Going off my instincts, I decided to do some detective work. I followed him on his day off. I saw him with the girl and two of his friends. He was holding hands with the girl. I stepped out and confronted him. He swore that the girl was his friend's cousin, and nothing was going on. He was lying to my face. I previously saw the girl at his mama's house when I went to visit his other best friend at his grandmother's house. I knew they had slept together because the girl's cousin (my boyfriend's friend) told me. Plus, he smelled just like her.

The girl decided to confront me and tried to fight me one day in front of our job. I had gone up there to get something to eat, and she was there kissing my boyfriend. I got in her face. All I remember was her swinging at me. The next thing I remember was being pulled off of her. I was so angry I didn't realize she had bitten me during the fight. I pulled my shirt off and was ready to go back and fight. I was held back, so I just left. To pay him back, I cheated on him with his best friend, then called my father to come to pick me up. I wanted him to hurt as much as I hurt. As my father drove away, he chased the truck, screaming my name. I refused to look back. Vindictive…probably. Did I care at the time? Nope!!

Chapter Three

I went back. It was stupid. I was stupid. I still kept thinking that he would change. For a little while, he did. He tried to pay me more attention. He tried to show me love. Now that I look back, his definition of love and mine were on two different ends of the spectrum. He kept making bad decisions. He ended up going to jail for doing something stupid. He got out on probation. I tried to help by taking the money I earned to help him pay for probation. $354 left, and he decides he doesn't want to pay anymore. Guess who went and paid the rest so he could get out of jail for violating probation? Yep, it was me. Again, I am aware that my teenage self made some really stupid decisions. Feel free to cuss, fuss, and say what you wouldn't have done. You were not me, nor did you have the mindset I did at that time.

    He got in trouble again. I was there for him again. I would visit him until income tax time to pay and get him out again. That was another issue in itself. His mama claimed he told her he would give her half of the money. The problem was, he and I had never had that conversation. I believe she was another person who tried to get over on me. Makes you wonder if that's where some of the deceitfulness came from. I wondered if I knew the cycle he was headed into and just didn't want to see it. I still thought I could get him to change though. I thought being a good and supportive girlfriend would make him want to be a better man. I was still wrong. Instead, he started back doing the same old things and making the same dumb decisions. He was finding ways to be more sneaky with the girls he was seeing. He would be gone for days sometimes, claiming that he was helping his stepfather with a job out of town. The man was covering for him too. I believe that they were covering each other when it came to cheating.

By that point, his mom didn't want me living with them anymore, so we had to find a place to go. We managed to rent the house across the street from his parents. I liked having our own space. I had more control. I was able to cook like I wanted to. I would still take the food over to his mom's house even though she made it known she didn't like me and wanted me to go back to my parent's house. She believed I was trying to sleep with her husband. It was the other way around.

Her husband was trying to sleep with me and had even made passes at me. I knew that man kept up a lot of mess and drama, especially with his girlfriend and wife on the side. Yes, I said it exactly how I meant it.

T   he only person that wasn't ever there was him. Yeah, he would go there for other things, but he never stuck around to spend time with me. My dad brought us a car so that we could get around. It was a wonderful gift. We took the car on its first trip to Fort Lauderdale, FL. We went to get his cousin and his cousin's girlfriend. It was great seeing another city with him. I don't think I was the company he wanted, though. Yet I enjoyed the trip anyway. I loved meeting his cousin and his cousin's girlfriend. They jumped in the car with us, and we were on our way back home. The conversation was great. I heard about him growing up and the antics he and his cousin used to pull. I also learned things about his past he never told me. I learned about a girl nicknamed Yoda, who was his first love. I now realized that I was competing for a heart that would never belong to me because it belonged to someone else. Found out that she was his first, not me. I was a replacement. My heart dropped as the conversation continued around me. I made up my mind that I could make him love me. I just needed to figure out how. By the way, the car broke down on the way back? Why? Because he wasn't car savvy. So he didn't check the coolant levels in the radiator, and the car overheated. Then he kept putting water in it instead of getting radiator fluid. First car together, gone from its first trip.

Chapter Four

We arrived home and began unpacking his cousin and his girlfriend. We gave them the second room since it wasn't being used. They were happy to be there with us. I was happy to have company so I wouldn't feel so alone. My boyfriend started working again, so I was lonely when he wasn't there. He did get me a rabbit as a pet which I loved. I had my first touchable pet. I grew up having pet fish, but it wasn't the same. That rabbit hid everywhere and left its pellets anywhere. I did a lot of cleaning behind that rabbit.

His cousin got a job also, so me and his girlfriend spent a lot of time together. At one point, we both thought we were pregnant, but once again, thankfully, we weren't. I don't think we were ready to treasure a little person yet, even though I did want to be a mom. I believed that a child would make our relationship better. Yet, it wasn't meant to happen at that time.

I thought it would make him change.

Little did I know the things to come…

I still believe I wanted more than he did from our relationship. That's when things began to change. He started saying things to me that were hurtful. He told me no one else would love me or want me but him. Then he would turn around and say how much he loved me and would never let me go. His cousin and his cousin's girlfriend ended up moving back to Florida. When they left, he decided he wanted to experiment with our relationship. He asked me for a threesome. Yep!! And guess what my idiot behind did? Grant his request with one catch. He picked his girl, and I could turn around and pick my guy. What I didn't know was the girl he picked he was already having sex with and had already discussed everything with her. By this point I was 18, so now it was just plain stupidity. He got his wish, and again I used one of his friends as payback. I tried to commit suicide a few days later because I felt so guilty and unwanted. I was giving him everything, and felt like I was losing who I was because of it. I didn't want to be with him anymore, but I felt like I couldn't go home either. I wear the scar on my wrist to remind me there is nothing I can do so bad that it's worth taking my life. A few days after that, this man pops up with Gonorrhea. Yep. He caught an STD from the girl. I blessedly was clean.

No more games for me after that. Didn't seem to change his mindset though.

While going through this, we lost our place because he wasn't paying the rent like he claimed he was. We had to find somewhere else to move to. We ended up moving in with his best friend's grandmother. It wasn't far from his mom's house. I realized that his mom was just how more important to him than I was. I would eventually find out just how much.

During this time, my papa died. He and the rest of my family had been trying to get me to go back home, but none of them understood what had happened and why I didn't want to go back. My mom had become abusive during her mental breakdown. I was the one who caught the worst of it. I would go to hell and back before I allowed myself to be treated that way again. My papa was my heart. He was the only grandfather I knew. My other grandfather died when I was 5, so all

I remembered of him was his funeral. I screamed when they took my papa's casket out of the church. Life seemed to just be piling on with no stops in sight.

He was back to his old ways. He was being sneaky and leaving to go places I didn't know about. I had a feeling he was cheating again; I just couldn't prove it. I hated when my heart would tell me one thing, but I would listen to my mind instead. My mind told me I couldn't prove anything, so nothing was going on. My heart knew better. Eventually, he found a place for us to stay. I was glad to have privacy again. We did find time for privacy while at his friend's grandma's house, but it was in a car, pulled off on some side road. Yes, he purchased a car for us. More hell was about to break loose from that too.

He got in trouble again and ended up in jail. While he was there, I was starting to feel sick. I decided to go to the Social Services office and have a pregnancy test done. I walked up there with his mom. I did the urine sample and waited patiently. I was called back in and told I was pregnant. I couldn't believe it. A baby that could change our lives was growing inside me. I just knew in my mind that this was going to make him grow up and change. My heart told me I was being stupid again. I immediately told his mom, who was excited about her first grandchild. I couldn't wait until my phone call with him so that I could tell him.

What I didn't know was that another girl was pregnant, and he was supposed to be the father. He was friends with her before he was incarcerated. He would take her and her children places. I tried not to think too much of it since he was helping someone at his job who was going through an abusive situation. Or so he told me. The lies were told so easily by him. So, one day, I went to his mother's friend's house to talk to him on the phone. I got on the phone for my phone call, not realizing that the other girl was listening on another line. I was telling him how excited I was about the pregnancy, and he was telling me how he couldn't believe it and how happy he was. I thought things between us were going to change now that we had created a life together. I was so much more wrong than I knew. The other girl suddenly butts into the conversation, saying how he promised to treasure and take care of their baby and promised her he would be there for her. Things started to make sense. He had been working at the job he had for four months, and the girl was four months pregnant. Things began to dawn on me. All the time he was spending away supposedly helping a "friend". The girl was married, and yet he was still messing with her. I heard her end of the conversation and him telling her the same lies he was telling me. I was broken. I couldn't believe that he would lie like that. Then again, he had lied before. I realized he was a pathological liar. I was hoping that the baby would change his ways. Now he probably would never change. After the phone call, the girl tried to attack me. The fight was broken up, but I realized that this girl was willing to put her baby and mine in danger over him. No matter what, I was not going to lose my baby over jealousy of her. My boyfriend nor her were with it.

Chapter Five

I spent the majority of my pregnancy alone since he was incarcerated still. I found out we were having a boy while he was gone. I also was locked up in the process because he stole some rims and left them on our porch. I was charged with receiving stolen property, even though I didn't even know they were stolen. My father paid my bail for me to get out, and I began building a relationship with my family again. I would spend weekends at their house. It was nice to be back with my family again. My mom would spoil me and take me to my appointments. My dad and I started talking again. I missed my relationship with my family. I even missed my annoying little brother. I think he was looking forward to being an uncle. He had a girlfriend, friends, and a job occupying his time, but he always made time to spend with me. It was like I had never lost my family, but the dynamics had changed.

I could tell that my family was breaking apart. Yet, it was something I didn't want to think about. I wanted to believe that things would change, but my heart knew they wouldn't. I knew that my dad and mom were breaking up. It was just a matter of when.

The charges against me were dropped, thankfully. I went home from visiting my family to go back to jail again. This time for stealing checks that I never touched. During that time, my boyfriend finally got out of jail. He somehow posted my bail, and I was free again. By this time, I was seven months pregnant. It was time to settle things and do things the right way. I bugged my boyfriend and even told him I would pay for us to get married to be a family before the baby came. He eventually agreed, and we got married on August 26. I just knew that marriage was going to change him. Now he was with me for life with us having a baby.

STUPID!!! The idiotic thoughts of a young mind.

   Once again, he changed for a little while, but he started going back to some of his old ways. He would disappear for hours. I had no way of reaching him except when he was at work. I was afraid I would go into labor alone and with no one to help me. He began coming home smelling like a perfume I didn't know. I felt like he was cheating on me again. I was praying to God that he wasn't, but my heart knew better. His cousin Red started taking me for walks to her house to get exercise and walk our son down. She had us walking almost 3 miles every day. She was pregnant herself and was getting her exercise in. One day, when we came back from walking, I began to feel sharp pains in my stomach. At first, I brushed them off as just pain from walking, but they didn't let up. I figured a warm bath would help, but the pain got worse. I realized I had gone into labor. There was no way to reach my husband, so his cousin had to call my mom and the ambulance. The pains were getting closer together, and they hurt badly. My husband's stepfather came by our house. I didn't want him anywhere near me. I just told him to let his son know that I was on the way to the hospital. The ambulance finally arrived I was on my way to the hospital.

Chapter Six

Six hours later, I had a beautiful baby boy in my arms. I was cussing and fussing through the whole ordeal. My mother fussed at me, but I didn't care. I had to have an episiotomy in the process. My husband showed up towards the end of the labor and almost missed our son being born. Our son was so handsome. He was 6lbs 12oz. He was so juicy. I couldn't believe that someone so beautiful had come from my body. My husband stood there just smiling away. I don't know what was going through his mind, but I hoped it was good. I wanted my son to have the same type of love from his father I had from mine, one who would be there for him no matter what. My husband kept saying he wanted to be a better father than his stepfather and biological father. Yeah, that was wishful thinking.

Then I realized my husband smelled like that perfume again. I knew why he hadn't been there for me through the whole labor. He had been with someone else. It seemed like nothing would change him. He wanted me to be his number one chick but wanted other women on the side. My heart broke into a million pieces. Nothing was going to change. I put myself in a situation that I couldn't get out of. I was stuck with a man who didn't want me as much as I thought he did. And nowhere near how much I wanted and loved him. Now I had to live with it. I placed myself in the situation, and I was going to see it through for the sake of my son.

I knew that freedom was not an option at that point. Now, this was what was going on in my mind. I know better than that now. I was so caught up in changing him that I let myself get trapped in his web of lies and deceit. My mind began shutting down. I focused my eyes on my son and realized that he was all I had in this relationship. How was I going to tell my family what I was going through? How was I going to say I needed help? Who would let me and a newborn baby stay with them? He hadn't started physically abusing me yet, but how long until he did? Are we safe with him? I was going to find out, and not the way I wanted to.

Chapter Seven

We arrived home from the hospital. I had to find a way to fill time because he never came home. He would go to work, come home and shower, then leave again. He would come home, shower, then go to work. My son had colic for about 2 weeks. Those were the longest 2 weeks of my life. Four weeks after having the baby, I had to work again. I had no choice. No money was coming in from where he was working, at least not that he was bringing home. I would leave my son with my husband, but someone was having some behind-the-scenes play.

One day, we went to a person's house I had never seen before to pick up my son after I had gotten off of work. He told the girl that my son was his little cousin. His son. I realized he had his other woman taking care of my son. I was in disbelief. My soul was crushed again. I didn't speak to him for the day. We eventually had to move again because we lost our place. After all, the rent was not being paid. As my dad was helping us move, the same girl pulled up in her car and ran to our house. She came straight to me and told me to get myself checked. My husband had given her gonorrhea, and that he may have given it to me. I knew he hadn't, because we hadn't had sex in a while. But my shock was still there. The house we were moving into used to be hers. I wanted to throw up. I could see the look in my father's eyes—sympathy for me, yet anger at my situation. I just wanted to crawl into a hole and die.

One day, I began fussing with him about being with other women and questioning why he kept cheating on me. He turned around, and he slapped me. That was the first time he hit me. As my head snapped to the side, I went into shock. I couldn't believe he had put his hands on me. I checked on my son and promised myself he would never put his hands on me again. I was so wrong.

Suddenly, there was this cousin that needed somewhere to stay. I knew there was something wrong with the issue, but he moved her in against my pleas not to. I knew he was sleeping with her. They would leave at night to go places, and they would come back smiling and laughing together. I knew she wasn't his cousin. He still lied to me and told me she was just his cousin.

One day, he and I argued. I wanted to take our son and leave. He wouldn't let me. He gave our son his "cousin" and told her to leave with him. I began to fight then. He wouldn't let me past him. He laughed at me, trying to pass him until I threw something at him. Then he began swinging at me. As he punched me, I started with everything in me to fight back to no avail. He knew where to hit me. He didn't leave any bruises that could be easily seen. Yet what he did bruised my soul.

He eventually had my son brought back. I cried my heart out. I realized that he would do anything to hurt me. I needed to get out. But how? We had an appointment at the WIC office. I felt if there was any way to get free, it was the Social Service office. When we pulled off, we were arguing. He wouldn't let me drive. We argued so badly that I jumped out of the car and went to grab my son. He grabbed him first and wouldn't give him to me. He was so forceful that he pushed me into a ditch, where l hit my head on the drain.

He looked at me while holding my son, knowing that there was nothing I could do, knowing he could intentionally hurt him. He made sure the cut was covered up before we left the house. He told me that if I ever left him, he would take my son so far away I would never find him. I knew the people in the office noticed my injury, but my husband made a point to hold our son the whole time, so I never got the chance to say anything. I was crushed. I wasn't going to get free. My heart sank to my feet.

Eventually, he and his "cousin" started robbing several fast food and convenience stores. They thought it was fun and funny, especially considering she looked a lot like me. One day, after I had dropped off my husband's sister and brother, I walked in to find him and the girl having sex in our bed, with my son lying next to the bed in his bassinet crying.

I was so angry. I got a knife out of the kitchen. I think if I hadn't snapped back, I would have killed both of them. God made away though. My husband was again locked up, this time for not missing court while out on bail. As soon as he was gone, I kicked homegirl out. You are not going to stay telling my son to call you mama. You crossed the line darling. Also, you don't get to play in my face with my husband. The horns had come out.

Chapter Eight

Eventually, I moved out of the house and into a place where it was easier to take care of my son and myself. My son reached his first birthday, and I had a really good job. I had started seeing someone who worked with me. I don't know how, but my husband found out about him and ruined everything. On top of that, he lied to the police and said that I helped him with two of the armed robberies I mentioned earlier so I would lose my son. That's exactly what happened. My baby was in foster care for 6 months.

I sat in jail for three months while my husband and his girlfriend waited to be convicted. It was the longest three months of my life. My dad made sure I had a good lawyer who made sure that my alibi was tight, which I knew it would be. I never participated in any of the armed robberies. I didn't even want to. My son and my life meant more to me than some quick money. I never knew a person could hate you so much that he intentionally got you locked up, so he could try to get his girlfriend to raise the child. While I sat in that cell, I realized that I was useful to him. I was the steak, but he wanted his mashed potatoes too. When I got out, I cut off all contact. I fought hard to get back custody of my son because the state was going to allow the people who had him to adopt him. I was not having that. My son meant everything to me. He was the only good thing that came out of that relationship. Later that year I went into the military. I needed a way to get myself and my son out of that town. I did not want the sins of the father to follow the son. The year after that I filed for divorce. I walked away with my son but also walked away with PTSD, depression, bipolar 1, and anxiety. From that point, I had the hardest time with men and relationships. I never gave up on love though. I later thought I thought I finally had Mr. Right. But he was Mr. Dead Wrong.

Epilogue

I know everyone thinks this girl should have said something but put yourself in her shoes. Feeling like you're stuck. Attached in a way you can't get out of. Domestic violence is so real. So many feel like they're stuck, especially when children are involved. Some get away. The only other way out for some is when the abuser kills them. You always think that you can change the person. You can't. It's better to get out. Call the police, call your family, call someone.

What happens is not your fault. You didn't

do anything wrong. You can be free.

Get Help

There are several ways to get help for abuse.

National Abuse Hotline 800-799-7233

There are also groups on Facebook and Instagram.

Narcissistic Abuse Helping Hands is one group on Facebook that helps.

Don't stay any longer. Do what you need to do so you can leave. Your children and family deserve the best version of you. They need you to live.

Next Book

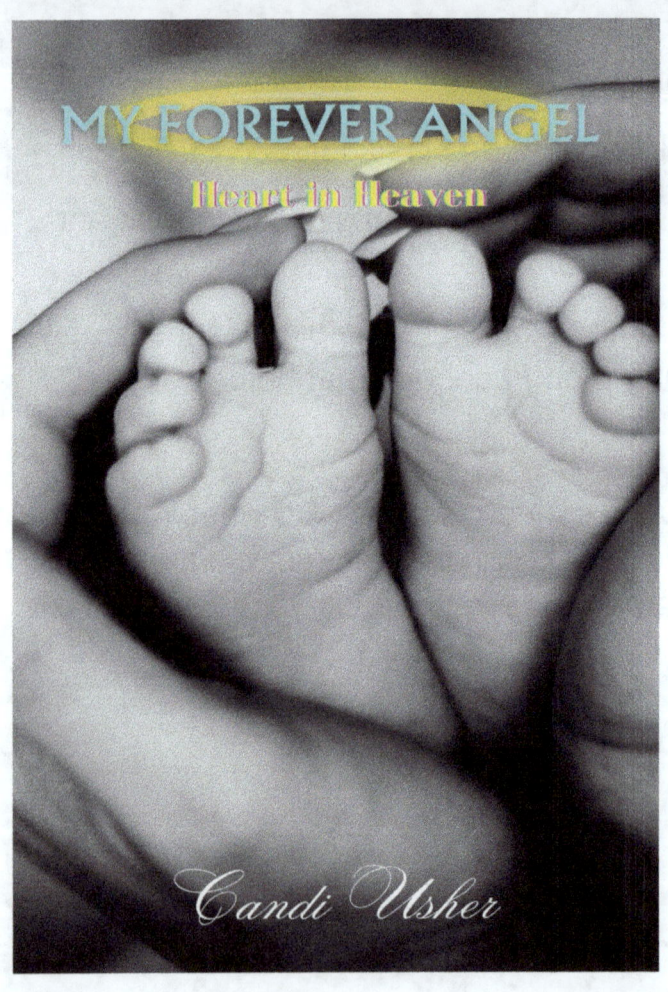

www.ingramcontent.com/pod-product-compliance
Lightning Source LLC
La Vergne TN
LVHW021953060526
838201LV00049B/1685